MARTIAL ARTS
JUJITSU

by Tim O'Shei

Reading Consultant:
Barbara J. Fox
Reading Specialist
North Carolina State University

Content Consultant:
Dennis Estes, Rokudan
Professor, Dan Zan Ryu Jujitsu
Shihan, American Judo and Jujitsu Federation
Medford, Oregon

Blazers is published by Capstone Press,
151 Good Counsel Drive, P.O. Box 669, Mankato, Minnesota 56002.
www.capstonepress.com

Library of Congress Cataloging-in-Publication Data
O'Shei, Tim.
    Jujitsu / by Tim O'Shei.
    p. cm. — (Blazers. Martial arts)
    Summary: "Discusses the history, techniques, ranks, and competitions of
jujitsu" — Provided by publisher.
    Includes bibliographical references and index.
    ISBN-13: 978-1-4296-1966-0 (hardcover)
    ISBN-10: 1-4296-1966-X (hardcover)
    1. Jiu-jitsu — Juvenile literature. I. Title.
GV1114.O817 2009
796.815'2 — dc22   2007052200

Essential content terms are **bold** and are defined on the spread where they first appear.

Editorial Credits
Abby Czeskleba, editor; Ted Williams, designer; Jo Miller, photo researcher;
    Sarah L. Schuette, photo shoot direction; Marcy Morin, scheduler

Photo Credits
All principle photography by Capstone Press/Karon Dubke except:
Alamy/Mary Evans Picture Library, 5; The Print Collector, 7
AP Images/Jack Mikrut, 25
Getty Images Inc./Bongarts/Christof Koepsel, 27

The Capstone Press Photo Studio thanks the members of the Harbor Lane Dojo
Club in Plymouth, Minnesota, for their assistance with this book.

1 2 3 4 5 6 13 12 11 10 09 08

TABLE OF CONTENTS

CHAPTER 1
THE BEGINNING OF JUJITSU

Hundreds of years ago, Japanese warriors carried deadly swords. These warriors were called samurai. They used their swords to fight off enemies during battles.

5

When the samurai dropped their swords, they fought with their hands and feet. The samurai and their enemies wore **armor.** The armor made it difficult to hurt each other.

armor — a covering worn by Japanese warriors for protection during battle

7

The samurai learned how to throw their enemies as a way to hurt them. Today, jujitsu fighters use some of the same skills the samurai used. Jujitsu is full of throws, punches, and pins.

MARTIAL ARTS FACT

U.S. soldiers were trained in jujitsu during World War II (1939–1945). Jujitsu was the first martial art to be brought to the United States.

CHAPTER 2
PRACTICING ON THE MAT

Jujitsu fighters wear a **gi**. They practice on mats. Fighters bow to each other before and after practices. Bowing shows respect for the other fighter.

gi — the pants and jacket worn by a jujitsu fighter

11

Fighters bend their knees and spread their feet. While fighting, they shift their weight between both feet. This foot positioning helps fighters move quickly.

MARTIAL ARTS FACT

Jujitsu fighters are called *jujitsuka*.

13

14

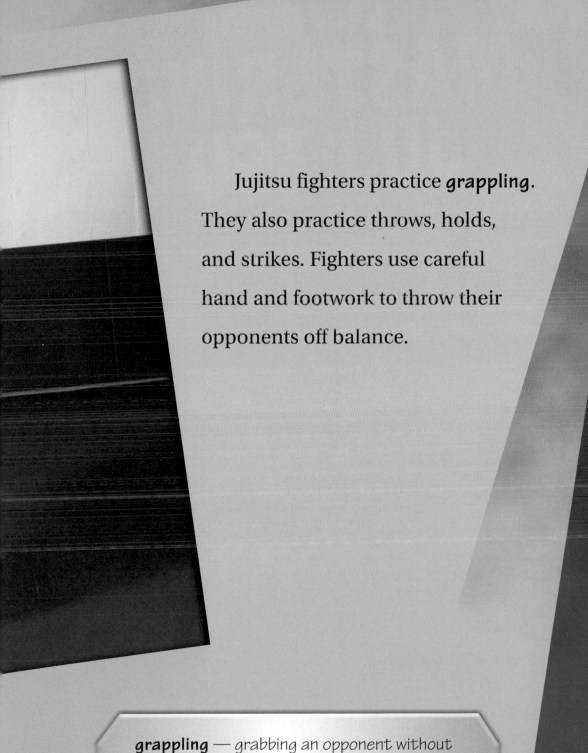

Jujitsu fighters practice **grappling**. They also practice throws, holds, and strikes. Fighters use careful hand and footwork to throw their opponents off balance.

grappling — grabbing an opponent without punching, kicking, or striking; wrestling is a grappling sport.

CHAPTER 3
MASTERING JUJITSU

Beginning jujitsu students wear white belts. As they learn new skills, they earn different belts. Beginning students have the rank of *kyu*. Jujitsu has up to 10 levels of kyu.

MARTIAL ARTS FACT

There are eight different colored belts in jujitsu.

Brown and blue belts are two of the eight
colored belts jujitsu fighters can earn.

After students pass the kyu levels, they earn the rank of *dan*. Jujitsu has 10 dan levels. A dan student wears a black belt. It usually takes a year or more to move up each black belt level. Most people never reach the **judan** level.

judan — the highest dan level; a judan student is a 10th degree black belt.

Kyu and dan students practice new moves. A skilled fighter can throw a bigger opponent. The smaller fighter uses the bigger fighter's weight. When the bigger fighter pulls, the smaller one pushes. Sometimes the bigger fighter goes flying!

JUJITSU DIAGRAM

BLACK BELT

22

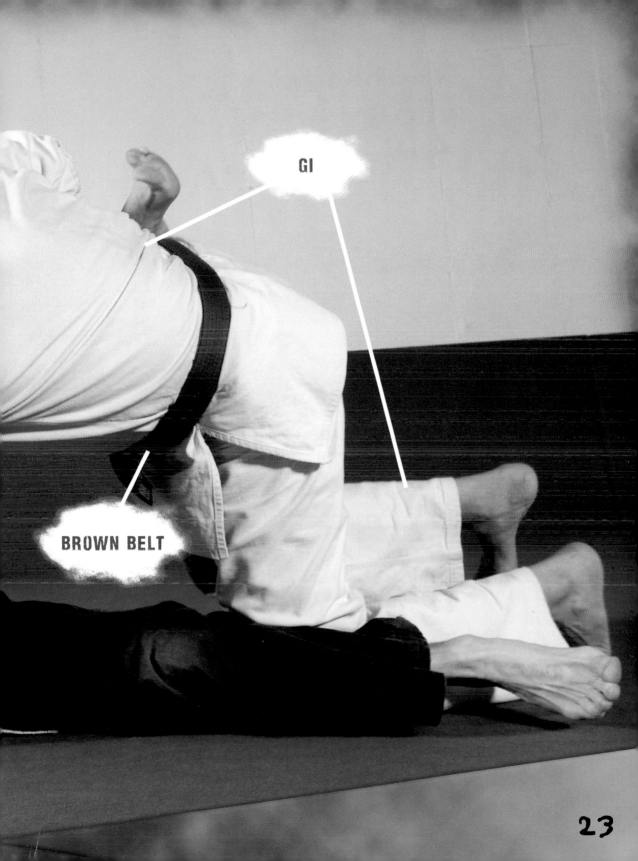

GI

BROWN BELT

23

CHAPTER 4
JUJITSU COMPETITIONS

Fighters compete in **weight classes.** They earn points for landing hits. Judges also award points for good throws. The fighter with the most points at the end of three rounds wins the match.

weight class — a group of jujitsu fighters who are the same weight; fighters who are in the same weight class compete one-on-one against each other.

The **World Games** happen every four years. In jujitsu, the top three fighters are awarded the gold, silver, and bronze medals. Jujitsu fighters continue to use the skills of the samurai from so long ago.

MARTIAL ARTS FACT

More than 15 countries competed in jujitsu at the 2005 World Games in Duisburg, Germany.

World Games — a competition with 32 sports; the sports include bowling, surfing, hockey, and martial arts.

27

ELBOW STRIKE!

GLOSSARY

armor (AR-muhr) — a covering worn by Japanese warriors for protection during battle

bow (BOU) — to bend low as a sign of respect

gi (GHEE) — the pants and jacket worn by a jujitsu fighter

grappling (GRAP-ling) — grabbing an opponent without punching, kicking, or striking; wrestling is a grappling sport.

judan (JU-dan) — the highest dan level; a judan student is a 10th degree black belt.

match (MACH) — a game or sporting competition; three rounds equal a match in jujitsu.

opponent (uh-POH-nuhnt) — a person who competes against another person in a fight or contest

weight class (WATE KLAS) — a group of jujitsu fighters who are the same weight; fighters who are in the same weight class compete one-on-one against each other.

World Games (WURLD GAMES) — a competition with 32 sports; the sports include bowling, surfing, hockey, and martial arts.

READ MORE

Buckley, Thomas. *Judo.* Kids' Guides to Martial Arts. Chanhassen, Minn.: Child's World, 2004.

Crossingham, John, and Bobbie Kalman. *Judo In Action.* Sports in Action. New York: Crabtree, 2006.

Johnson, Nathan. *Jujutsu: Essential Tips, Drills, and Combat Techniques.* Martial and Fighting Arts. Broomall, Penn: Mason Crest, 2003.

INTERNET SITES

FactHound offers a safe, fun way to find Internet sites related to this book. All of the sites on FactHound have been researched by our staff.

Here's how:
1. Visit *www.facthound.com*
2. Choose your grade level.
3. Type in this book ID **142961966X** for age-appropriate sites. You may also browse subjects by clicking on letters, or by clicking on pictures and words.
4. Click on the **Fetch It** button.

FactHound will fetch the best sites for you!

INDEX